Presented to

By

Date

Occasion

About My Father's Business

ALSO BY JANICE N. ADAMS

About My Father's Footsteps

A Heart's Journey: To Quench a Thirsty Soul

A Twisted State of Mind
(Contribution to Another Time, Another Place)

EDITED BY JANICE N. ADAMS

About My Father's Business

About My Father's Footsteps

A Heart's Journey: To Quench a Thirsty Soul

About My Father's Business

A Book of Inspiration

by

Janice N. Adams

JAVISTA BOOKS

New York   London   Toronto

JAVISTA BOOKS
43 Randolph Road, #322
Silver Spring, MD 20904

Copyright © 2009 by Janice N. Adams

All rights reserved. No part of this publication may be reproduced, stored in a retrieval system, or transmitted in any form or by any means (electronic, mechanical, photocopying, recording, or otherwise) without written permission from the publisher, excepting brief quotes used in printed reviews. For information address JAVISTA BOOKS, 43 Randolph Rd., #322, Silver Spring, MD 20904.

ISBN-13: 978-0-9814521-2-8
ISBN-10: 0-9814521-2-4

Library of Congress Control Number: 2008938483

First Printing: March 2009
10 9 8 7 6 5 4 3 2 1

Scripture quotations in this book are from the Holy Bible, *New International Version*, copyright 1973, 1978, 1984 by International Bible Society.

Cover and interior photographed by Microsoft Corporation
Cover design by Janice N. Adams
Manufactured in the United States of America

This edition is printed on acid-free paper.

For
Andi, LaTeshia, and Shirley

Contents

A Witness, a Warning, and a Wonder 1
Out of the Flesh and Into the Spirit 3
You Have to Walk Before You Fly 6
Finishing Your Course with Joy 9
Genuine Commitment 12
You Will Because You Must 15
A Powerful Habit 17
Advice for Serious Depression 20
The Right Road 24
Go Get Your Purpose 26
What Satan Can't Stand 29
Unity 32
God's Grace 34
It's Time for a Change 37
A Better Day 41
So Great Salvation 44
Seize Your Moment 47
Go Deep 50
A Shepherd on a Mission 53
Resolving Family Conflict 56
It's Time to Eat 60

Hard But Not Impossible	*63*
The Resurrection of Christ	*66*
I Woke Up This Morning	*70*
Marching Feet in the Treetops	*73*
Antidote for Anxiety	*76*
APPENDIX 1: Discussion Questions	*81*
APPENDIX 2: Prayer Tables	*83*
APPENDIX 3: Intercessory Prayer List	*85*
APPENDIX 4: Spiritual Resources	*87*
APPENDIX 5: References	*88*

Introduction

Thank you, God, for blessing me with my third publication. You have shown me such grace and favor. I pray that You are pleased with my efforts to continue to serve You and spread your joy to others.

I extend a special thanks to Erica Wigley and Yasmin Miller; what would I have done without you? I sincerely appreciate your time and dedication to this project. Thank you a million times over for your involvement and willingness to help. Your insight is fantastic. To my family and friends who continue to support my writing, I sincerely appreciate your kind words and encouragement. To my readers, thank you for wanting to experience a different flavor of my writing.

Several people have asked me, how did I come up with the idea for this book? Here's what happened. I started taking notes in church about seventeen years ago because I wanted to reflect on God's word in my everyday life. I figured having my notes as a point of reference, in addition to the Bible, would help me through the coming weeks, especially when challenges arose.

One day, I decided to put together a compilation of my notes. I started the collection years ago, and then somewhere along the way, I placed my project in a drawer where it sat for four years until now. What made me revisit my project? God said that it was time.

During the summer of 2008, two of my friends informed me that they were diagnosed with breast cancer and were undergoing chemotherapy. Needless to say I was shocked and saddened. Hearing their news brought the total count of my friends with breast cancer to three. At that time, all three were under the age of forty-five. I felt helpless and wondered what I could do to help them. I gave them each other's email addresses, so they could support one another, but I never felt like that was enough and continued to feel uneasy over the weeks.

Then late one night after working all day and night on my first novel, *A Heart's Journey: To Quench a Thirsty Soul*, I went to bed completely exhausted; it was about four thirty a.m. All I wanted was a good night's sleep. Lying there beneath my sheets with a headache that would not quit, I tossed and turned, praying that God would give me rest, but He didn't. Images and thoughts about my collection of sermon notes circled about my mind while I whispered, "Lord, just let me sleep; I'm so tired." But He didn't. Images of the book cover, title, and marketing ideas for the book bolted through my mind. I continued to toss and turn while my headache intensified. My eyes watered from the pain and I continued to plead with the Lord to let me sleep. But He didn't. Images of my friends with breast cancer and what I could do to help them and many women like them flowed through my mind. Finally I said, "Okay, Lord, I'll do it. I'll finish the book of inspiration and give a portion of the proceeds from book sales to the Breast Cancer Research Foundation." Only then did He grant me rest and I fell soundly asleep.

Early the next morning, I felt a sense of urgency and immediately started working on the book. During that week, I designed and completed the first draft of *About My Father's Business* in support of my friends, Andi, LaTeshia, and Shirley. I then handed the manuscript to one of my proofreaders and received her comments back a couple of weeks later. Soon afterwards, Andi became ill and was admitted to the hospital. The day I visited her was the first and last opportunity I was given to share the document with her. She was surprised and ecstatic to see the manuscript and learn of my dedication to her and the others. I'm so glad that I gave her those moments of joy. I wish Andi was here today to share in the release of *their* book, but God called her home soon after my visit. It was then that I understood why God gave me a sense of urgency.

Readers, as you turn the pages of my memoirs, please understand that I am not an expert on the Bible or Theology. I am like millions of regular folks who attend church and want to apply the lessons learned from the service to everyday life. I recorded my spiritual notes to aide in enhancing my relationship with God. The notes enable me to reflect on His word and the teachings of Jesus

Christ. My notes are a combination of themes and content from the spoken word of pastors who are referenced in the appendices, my interpretation of their messages, and my examination of biblical scripture.

Each day is a blessing and an opportunity to do more and be more than we were the previous day. This book is my way of supporting a worthy cause and bringing words of inspiration to you as my Father in Heaven instructed. The quoted scripture at the beginning of each memoir is a small portion of the NIV biblical text associated with each title. I urge you to read the full scripture for completion and understanding.

I truly hope you enjoy the book and understand that its purpose is intended to help you with your spiritual growth and awareness, regardless of whether you are a Christian or not. The text is structured around Christianity because I am Baptist. However, there is something to be gained in the midst of these pages for anyone's wellbeing. The compilation is more than my memoirs; it's about my Father's business to reach out to you.

Peace and Blessings,

Janice

A WITNESS, A WARNING, AND A WONDER

"There came a man who was sent from God; his name was John. He came as a witness to testify concerning that light, so that through him all men might believe. He himself was not the light; he came only as a witness to the light. The true light that gives light to every man was coming into the world. He was in the world, and though the world was made through him, the world did not recognize him. He came to that which was his own, but his own did not receive him. Yet to all who received him, to those who believed in his name, he gave the right to become children of God - children born not of natural descent, nor of human decision or a husband's will, but born of God."

John 1:6-13

A man named John (i.e., John the Baptist) was sent from God. John came as a witness to testify about the Light of the World and that through the Light of the World, all men might believe. He warned people that they should believe in the Light. Yet when the

Light of the World physically came into the world, only certain people received Him and believed in His name. To those people, the Light of the World gave a wonder. He gave them the right to become children of God.

The Light of the World is Jesus Christ. He wants a witness. He gives you a wonder by blessing you when you receive Him. Don't overlook or underestimate Jesus because with Him nothing is impossible.

> **KEY POINT:** Establish a relationship with Jesus Christ.

QUESTIONS TO ASK YOURSELF:

1. How will you be a witness for Jesus Christ?

_____
_____
_____

2. What do you need to restore in your life in order to receive Him completely?

_____
_____
_____

3. What is in your life that seems impossible? What is your plan to address it?

_____
_____
_____

About My Father's Business

OUT OF THE FLESH AND INTO THE SPIRIT

"And if the Spirit of him who raised Jesus from the dead is living in you, he who raised Christ from the dead will also give life to your mortal bodies through his Spirit who lives in you. Therefore, brothers, we have an obligation - but it is not to the sinful nature, to live according to it. For if you live according to the sinful nature, you will die; but if by the Spirit you put to death the misdeeds of the body, you will live, because those who are led by the Spirit of God are sons of God. For you did not receive a spirit that makes you a slave again to fear, but you received the Spirit of sonship. And by him we cry, "Abba, Father.""

Romans 8:11-15

"In the same way, the Spirit helps us in our weakness. We do not know what we ought to pray for, but the Spirit himself intercedes for us with groans that words cannot express. And he who searches our hearts knows the mind of the Spirit because the Spirit intercedes for the saints in accordance with God's will."

Romans 8:26-27

The flesh is the nature of a person that fights with the Spirit of God. The flesh has nothing to offer you, but the Spirit of God has everything. Put to rest the sinful nature and misdeeds of the body and be led by the Spirit of God. You will receive the Spirit of "sonship" because we are God's children. Understand that the Spirit helps us in our weakness. If you don't know what to pray for in your moments of weakness, ask the Spirit to intercede and it will.

As part of your fellowship with God and through glory (i.e., Jesus), you can be delivered from your suffering. Jesus suffered on the cross for our sins and salvation, but glory to God, Jesus conquered death and rose from the dead. The Holy Spirit lives in believers now. Just like Jesus, you may have to go through some suffering, but glory is on the way and the difficult times will pass. There are two tools to help you through difficult times, hope and faith.

- <u>Hope</u> is the expectation. Hope gives you something to hold onto as you seek better circumstances; it's the vision in your mind.

- <u>Faith</u> is the surety in knowing that what you hope for will come to fruition.

Fellowship with the Holy Ghost is to have a partnership with God. With such a partnership, you have a place for your hope and faith.

KEY POINT: Live your life by the Spirit of God.

QUESTIONS TO ASK YOURSELF:

1. What misdeeds do you need to put to rest in order to

About My Father's Business

receive the sonship of God?

_____
_____
_____

2. What suffering are you currently experiencing?

_____
_____
_____

3. What do you hope for? How strong is your faith in order to receive what you hope for?

_____
_____
_____

YOUR EMOTIONS:
*How do you feel right now?
Why do you feel this way?*

_____
_____
_____

Janice N. Adams

YOU HAVE TO WALK BEFORE YOU FLY

"Be imitators of God, therefore, as dearly loved children and live a life of love, just as Christ loved us and gave himself up for us as a fragrant offering and sacrifice to God."
Ephesians 5:1-2

"For you were once darkness, but now you are light in the Lord. Live as children of light (for the fruit of the light consists in all goodness, righteousness and truth) and find out what pleases the Lord."
Ephesians 5:8-10

"Be very careful, then, how you live – not as unwise but as wise, making the most of every opportunity, because the days are evil. Therefore do not be foolish, but understand what the Lord's will is."
Ephesians 5:15-17

About My Father's Business

Walk like a child of God. Be an imitator of God and live a life of love just as Jesus Christ loved us and sacrificed Himself for us. Be motivated in your walk with a sacrificial love of Jesus Christ. Walk in truth. Children of God consist of goodness, righteousness, and truth. Be careful how you live. Love as a wise person. Do not be foolish but understand what the Lord's will is for you in all things. Walk in a manner that is pleasing to God. Don't let bad experiences sour you. Let sweetness lead you.

You have to kneel before you walk. Be humble and kneel in prayer to start your day. We need to recognize God. The Lord hears the humble. Identify and take control over whatever concerns you, in His Name. If you feel oppressed, trust that the Lord is righteous and will set you free. Pray, and then start your day. We walk by faith. Like a child learning to walk to parents, God is at the end, holding out His arms for us to come to Him. Prayer allows you to go to God and release your thoughts and/or feelings. Prayer frees you from burdens and allows you to be renewed by God.

> **KEY POINT:** Love others the way Christ loves you.

QUESTIONS TO ASK YOURSELF:

1. Are you living a life of goodness, righteousness, and truth? If yes, explain how. If not, what is stopping you?

_____
_____
_____

2. What bad experiences are you holding onto that you need

to release and turn over to God?

_____
_____
_____

3. What lifestyle changes will you make to improve your time with God?

_____
_____
_____

ADDITIONAL SELF-REFLECTION:
What's on Your Mind?

_____
_____
_____
_____
_____

About My Father's Business

FINISHING YOUR COURSE WITH JOY

"I have declared to both Jews and Greeks that they must turn to God in repentance and have faith in our Lord Jesus. "And now, compelled by the Spirit, I am going to Jerusalem, not knowing what will happen to me there. I only know that in every city the Holy Spirit warns me that prison and hardships are facing me. However, I consider my life worth nothing to me, if only I may finish the race and complete the task the Lord Jesus has given me - the task of testifying to the gospel of God's grace."
Acts 20:21-24

Everyone has a course and a task in life. A task is merely testifying about or bearing witness to a certain thing. A course is more difficult because generally, a person is not sure of his/her course. In order to be sure that we are on the right course, we must follow Jesus Christ.

The Apostle Paul was not sure of his course as he returned to Jerusalem, but suspected that prison and hardship awaited him. Yet, he was determined to go to the city anyway and finish the task Jesus gave him which was to testify to the gospel of God's grace. Paul went to Jerusalem how? Bound in the spirit of Christ.

You can face anything and stand your ground when you are bound in the spirit. Your course is God's business. The task (i.e., testifying) is your business. He that is in you is greater than he that is in the world. Stand your ground with God in you. Things such as persecution, ridicule, and loneliness have no real power over you because they are simply circumstances.

Be aware of your emotional state. When you allow yourself to be consumed by emotion, you cannot think clearly. Unstable emotions create a mind full of clutter. So often, it's during these times that people make irrational decisions. Stay conscious of your emotions at all times; they should not control your course, alter your aim, or steal your joy.

Receive your ministry from Christ. Then finish your course; realize your vision and finish with joy. You might cry, be misunderstood, or get depressed. It's all right for these things to happen, but make sure that you finish your course.

KEY POINT: Understand and achieve your life's course.

QUESTIONS TO ASK YOURSELF:

1. *Why you are here? How have you asked God to reveal your purpose?*

About My Father's Business

_____
_____
_____

2. What approach do you use to free your mind and soul of emotional clutter? Does this approach work? Why or why not?

_____
_____
_____

3. What emotions do you need to control right now? Why?

_____
_____
_____

YOUR EMOTIONS:
*How do you feel right now?
Why do you feel this way?*

_____
_____
_____

Janice N. Adams

GENUINE COMMITMENT

"As they approached Jerusalem and came to Bethphage and Bethany at the Mount of Olives, Jesus sent two of his disciples, saying to them, "Go to the village ahead of you, and just as you enter it, you will find a colt tied there, which no one has ever ridden. Untie it and bring it here. If anyone asks you, 'Why are you doing this?' tell him, 'The Lord needs it and will send it back here shortly.'" They went and found a colt outside in the street, tied at a doorway. As they untied it, some people standing there asked, "What are you doing untying that colt?" They answered as Jesus had told them to, and the people let them go."

Mark 11:1-6

About My Father's Business

If you are not genuinely committed to Christ, you will yield. Genuine commitment demands unquestionable obedience to spiritual authority and instruction just as when Jesus gave two disciples direct and specific instructions to go to the village ahead of them and bring Him back a colt. He warned the disciples that people would ask why were they taking the colt. Jesus instructed them to tell the people that they were taking the colt for the Lord. The disciples did as He asked without question and without concern about what the people might say or think.

Genuine commitment ultimately points to the glory of God. Become active agents to carry out the divine plan, God's plan. When there is genuine commitment, you are not concerned with thoughts of how others perceive you.

KEY POINT: You become whatever you are committed to.

QUESTIONS TO ASK YOURSELF:

1. How committed are you to Jesus Christ?

___

2. How have you allowed the thoughts of others to impact your commitment to Jesus?

___

3. What is your plan to increase your commitment to Christ?

_____
_____
_____

ADDITIONAL SELF-REFLECTION:
What's on Your Mind?

_____
_____
_____
_____
_____

About My Father's Business

YOU WILL BECAUSE YOU MUST

""You are not yet fifty years old," the Jews said to him, "and you have seen Abraham!" "I tell you the truth," Jesus answered, "before Abraham was born, I am!" At this, they picked up stones to stone him, but Jesus hid himself, slipping away from the temple grounds."
John 8:57-59

Jesus did not doubt or negotiate who He was or His relationship with God when the Jews questioned whether He was a Samaritan possessed with a demon. He remained obedient to God, even when the Jews wanted to stone Him because of His proclaimed relationship to God.

Everyone needs non-negotiables. Without these, you become a puppet of the ignorant majority (i.e., people drifting alone without a godly purpose or cause). You must develop godly ambitions. That is, you must have a mandate of divine purpose to pursue in your life.

What must you do or be? How do you determine your non-negotiables? The answer is to adopt Jesus' non-negotiables. Commit to the following three things:

1. Obeying Father God.
2. Seizing the moment by seeking God's kingdom first.
3. Honoring Jesus.

> **KEY POINT:** Godly ambitions yield divine purposes.

QUESTIONS TO ASK YOURSELF:

1. What divine purpose are you pursuing in your life?

_____
_____
_____

2. What are your non-negotiables? How are they aligned with God's principles?

_____
_____
_____

3. How will your Godly ambitions help you grow as a person?

_____
_____
_____

About My Father's Business

A POWERFUL HABIT

"Then Jesus told his disciples a parable to show them that they should always pray and not give up. He said: "In a certain town there was a judge who neither feared God nor cared about men. And there was a widow in that town who kept coming to him with the plea, 'Grant me justice against my adversary.' "For some time he refused. But finally he said to himself, 'Even though I don't fear God or care about men, yet because this widow keeps bothering me, I will see that she gets justice, so that she won't eventually wear me out with her coming! And the Lord said, "Listen to what the unjust judge says. And will not God bring about justice for his chosen ones, who cry out to him day and night? Will he keep putting them off? I tell you, he will see that they get justice and quickly. However, when the Son of Man comes, will he find faith on earth?"

Luke 18:1-8

Janice N. Adams

You should always pray and never give up because God will see to it that you get justice. But sometimes God makes us wait, just like the widow who constantly asked the judge to grant her justice against her adversary. An adversary is a person or thing that continues to get in the way of you accomplishing something good. For example, a person who pushes your buttons on purpose can be an adversary.

Likewise, sometimes when you find a solution, it doesn't mean that the solution is immediately available just like in the case of the widow. The judge was her solution, but for some time, he refused her request. Why did God delay coming to the widow's rescue? The problem wasn't with the judge or God. Sometimes God makes us wait until:

- Our motives are purified.
- Our desires are intensified.
- We learn patience.

So don't get discouraged; be persistent, and never give up. The widow developed a powerful habit in constantly going to the judge. Eventually, the judge granted her the justice she sought. Be persistent with your prayers; pray without ceasing. Develop a powerful habit in going to Jesus. God will come to help you because you are his chosen people. Remember that every day God has compassion.

KEY POINT: Never stop praying.

QUESTIONS TO ASK YOURSELF:

1. What have you been praying for that seems like God hasn't

answered?

2. Why do you think God has not answered your prayer? What do you believe He is teaching you?

3. In your patience for God to answer your prayer, how persistent are you praying in the meantime?

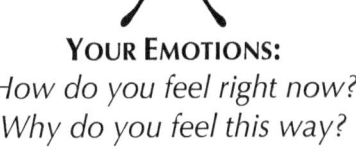

YOUR EMOTIONS:
*How do you feel right now?
Why do you feel this way?*

Janice N. Adams

ADVICE FOR SERIOUS DEPRESSION

"Elijah was afraid and ran for his life. When he came to Beersheba in Judah, he left his servant there, while he himself went a day's journey into the desert. He came to a broom tree, sat down under it and prayed that he might die. "I have had enough, Lord," he said. "Take my life; I am no better than my ancestors." Then he lay down under the tree and fell asleep. All at once an angel touched him and said, "Get up and eat."

1 Kings 19:3-5

Elijah felt alone because the Israelites rejected God's covenant and killed God's prophets. Elijah thought he was the only one left who was zealous for God. He ran from the Israelites, afraid that they wanted to kill him too. He was fatigued and felt like giving up, at which point he wanted God to take his life.

Depression comes from feeling overwhelmed. It results in hopelessness, worthlessness, meaninglessness, and sadness. You may do everything you know how to end your depression. For example, you may pray, fast, have family and friends pray for you, confess your sins, etc. but your spiritual slump may still exist, causing you to think that God has abandoned you. When God seems distant, you may experience emotions such as anger and disappointment. You may even feel as though He is punishing you. But this is not the case at all. God is simply testing your faith to determine if you will continue to love, trust, obey, and worship Him when you have no sense of His presence in your life. It is during these times that faith matures.

During bouts of depression, remember that God is omnipresent; He is always with you even when you think He is not. Additionally, sometimes your greatest victory can be followed by your greatest depression. However, you must understand the root causes of depression.

Three Root Causes of Depression:

1. <u>Fear</u> – Being afraid of not having resources (e.g., a job, a home, marriage, family, friends, etc.)

2. <u>Failure</u> – Having negative feelings about oneself. You must know who you are because others will manipulate you if you are unaware. Be confident and think more highly of yourself.

3. <u>Fatigue</u> – Feeling wearied and tired, wanting to give up.

When you have a better understanding of the root causes of depression, you can better address them. Try these biblical strategies.

Strategies to Battle Depression:

1. <u>Take Time Off</u> – Get physically and mentally rejuvenated by focusing on God's word. Put back the energy life steals from you. Get away from the daily routine, people, and pressures.

2. <u>Let It All Out</u> – Talk out your frustration. Sometimes we need someone to listen. God is always there to listen. He will never leave you. Take your burdens to the Lord and leave them there. Whether you cry, pray, sing, or shout it out, the main point is to let it out. In doing so, you are giving God permission to handle everything and as a result, you are able to live free of your frustrations because God has your back.

3. <u>Listen for the Lord</u> – Stop listening to your circumstances. Listen to God. Silence the noise around you and listen for God's voice. His voice will put you on the right path and lead to some form of positive action. Get up when you don't feel like it. Stand up against your circumstances. Through Jesus Christ, utilize your relationship with God.

> **KEY POINT:** Keep your faith in God.

QUESTIONS TO ASK YOURSELF:

1. What, if anything, do you feel depressed about?

_____
_____

2. What do you believe is the root cause of your depression?

About My Father's Business

How have you addressed the root cause?

_____
_____
_____

3. To what degree do you continue to love God during times of depression: somewhat, same, more? Explain.

_____
_____
_____

ADDITIONAL SELF-REFLECTION:
What's on Your Mind?

_____
_____
_____
_____
_____

Janice N. Adams

THE RIGHT ROAD

"Enter through the narrow gate. For wide is the gate and broad is the road that leads to destruction, and many enter through it. But small is the gate and narrow the road that leads to life, and only a few find it."
Matthew 7:13-14

On the road of life, have a sense of direction and destination. Decide how you are going to arrive at your destination. Every road must come to an end. The road of life will come to an end. The gate that is wide and the road that is broad leads to destruction. The gate that is small and the road that is narrow leads to life. Which road will you choose? Where will you spend your eternity, what will be your life's destination, heaven or hell? Follow the footprints God has set before you. Choose the right road with Jesus.

Consider the splendor of the earth. Look up at the sky at night and

About My Father's Business

see all the stars. Look during the day and see the blue sky and fluffy white clouds. If heaven is this beautiful on the bottom, imagine what it looks like on the top. If God created such beautiful things for us to see and enjoy, imagine what He will create for you if you will follow His lead down the right road.

KEY POINT: Follow the road of righteousness.

QUESTIONS TO ASK YOURSELF:

1. What destination do you seek in your walk of life?

___

2. What plans have you made to arrive spiritually at your destination?

___

3. Are you using good judgment and following God's lead down the right road? If yes, how? If not, why not?

___

Janice N. Adams

GO GET YOUR PURPOSE

"Listen to advice and accept instruction, and in the end you will be wise. Many are the plans in a man's heart, but it is the Lord's purpose that prevails."
Proverbs 19:20-21

Proverbs provides the structure for wisdom. It gives detailed instructions regarding how we should relate to and tackle various issues, situations, and people. The key word in Proverbs is wisdom, that is, living life skillfully and applying the things God teaches us about living in His kingdom.

People need a purpose in life in the body of Christ. Collisions occur because people don't know where they are going. We can be destructive to ourselves, and to others. You need to know your purpose. Nobody else can do that for you. Yield to God when others

About My Father's Business

try to tell you what they want you to do. People often have their own expectations of what you should do and most times they try to guide you into what they want. Only God can truly guide you.

Your purpose was in the mind of God before the world made you. Remember these three things:

1. <u>You are the only one who can fulfill your purpose.</u> Find out what it is, now. Discover your natural inclinations. For example, are you good with communication and generating ideas? Do you lead or follow others? God instilled in each of us our purpose before we were born. You ought to be fulfilling your purpose.

2. <u>The world is waiting for you to do what you were born to do.</u> Everything is related. When you don't do what you are supposed to do, it affects others. We are linked together. We have to come together, in the body of Christ. Everything is part of a larger picture.

3. <u>God is expecting His glory from you as you pursue it.</u> He will not be satisfied until you give in to your purpose.

> **KEY POINT:** Wisdom is learned and practiced skillfully.

QUESTIONS TO ASK YOURSELF:

1. What do you believe the world is waiting to receive from you?

_____
_____
_____

2. How will you use wisdom to help determine your life's purpose?

___
___
___

3. What are your expectations of yourself? How do they fit into fulfilling the glory of God?

___
___
___

YOUR EMOTIONS:
*How do you feel right now?
Why do you feel this way?*

___
___
___

About My Father's Business

WHAT SATAN CAN'T STAND

"Jesus, full of the Holy Spirit, returned from the Jordan and was led by the Spirit in the desert, where for forty days he was tempted by the devil. He ate nothing during those days, and at the end of them he was hungry. The devil said to him, "If you are the Son of God, tell this stone to become bread." Jesus answered, "It is written: 'Man does not live by bread alone.'" The devil led him up to a high place and showed him in an instant all the kingdoms of the world, and said to him, "I will give you all their authority and splendor, for it has been given to me, and I can give it to anyone I want to. So if you worship me, it will all be yours." Jesus answered, "It is written: 'Worship the Lord your God and serve him only.'"
Luke 4:1-8

Janice N. Adams

There is a presence in the world known as the devil. All of us are at risk and can fall prey to the devil. A saint (i.e., any believer in Christ) should not be enticed by temptation. If you are a child of God, there should not be periods of demonic inspired action. The works of your life ought to make demons stand outside your life. If you are a saint, then you should not struggle with moral and spiritual temptations. Periods of spiritual serenity should exist. And if you find yourself in the midst of a storm, your faith should not alter because when you truly believe in God, you know that all is well because God is in control.

Jesus went into the wilderness where for forty days, He was tempted by the devil. The devil appears when you're trying to do right and when you're at your lowest weak point. The devil plants seeds of doubt, which causes individuals to detour from their straight path. The devil sees our worship and gets busy trying to destroy it. But just like Jesus in the wilderness, we have a choice whether to keep temptation away.

Your spirit should be your authority not your body. God's spirit should be in you. If your thoughts are holy, then you won't waste time on unholy activities because your thoughts control your actions. If you want to rid a temptation, focus on something else because temptation always starts with a thought. Allow yourself to get interested in another idea, one that is pleasing to God.

The quality of your life brings about respect. Resist the devil and submit yourself to God and the devil will leave you alone. You are the domain of the Divine. The devil tried to make Jesus feel like He needed him. The devil wanted Jesus to worship him, but Jesus understood that only God receives such worship. Jesus' response was to worship then serve God. You must worship God before you serve Him. The devil tries to frustrate you so that you can't praise God. When you worship God, you see a difference in your life. Put all your trust in God. Learn how to praise the Lord. Praise the Lord no matter what.

> **KEY POINT:** Temptation is a choice.

QUESTIONS TO ASK YOURSELF:

1. What temptation have you experienced lately? Did you give into the temptation? Why or why not?

   _____
   _____
   _____

2. When do you think that you are most vulnerable to temptation? What good thoughts can you focus on to alter your mindset during moments of temptation?

   _____
   _____
   _____

3. How will you keep your thoughts holy so that your actions are holy?

   _____
   _____
   _____

Janice N. Adams

UNITY

"Is not the cup of thanksgiving for which we give thanks a participation in the blood of Christ? And is not the bread that we break a participation in the body of Christ? Because there is one loaf, we, who are many, are one body for we partake of the one loaf."
1 Corinthians 10:16-17

Communion is the union with God through which we partake as one body in Christ. We must have union with Christ and the church. Communion with Christ is a personal interaction with Him through meditation and prayer. He answers by granting us fresh thoughts and emotions. Our thoughts, views, and emotions are all ways by which we may communicate with Christ; this leads to

About My Father's Business

fellowship.

A soul with Christ that has been accepted by Him will have eternal life. No man or devil on earth can take Christ away from us. No other fellowship is more sincere than that with Christ. Seek Him because He is waiting for you to reach out to Him. Acknowledge Him and the sacrifice He made for our sins so that we may be unified with our Father in Heaven. Praise Him all the day long because He is worthy of our praise. There is no one on earth who loves you more than Jesus Christ. Live in the body of Christ.

KEY POINT: Fellowship with Jesus Christ.

QUESTIONS TO ASK YOURSELF:

1. What method do you use to communicate with Jesus? How often do you talk with Jesus?

___

2. How would you rate your relationship with Christ: poor, good, excellent? Explain.

___

3. How can you increase your fellowship with Him?

___

Janice N. Adams

GOD'S GRACE

"Praise be to the God and Father of our Lord Jesus Christ, who has blessed us in the heavenly realms with every spiritual blessing in Christ. For he chose us in him before the creation of the world to be holy and blameless in his sight. In love he predestined us to be adopted as his sons through Jesus Christ, in accordance with his pleasure and will - to the praise of his glorious grace, which he has freely given us in the One he loves. In him we have redemption through his blood, the forgiveness of sins in accordance with the riches of God's grace that he lavished on us with all wisdom and understanding."

Ephesians 1:3-8

About My Father's Business

Praise prepares us to get closer to God. When you give God praise, He will give you joy. Joy is the spirit of God that will carry you through hard times. The adversary (i.e., the devil) wants to steal your praise, so always remember to praise God through your circumstances. The devil lies to us. Call on God's grace, and let God know that you need Him. If you pray, God will give you grace. Grace will bring you what you need. When you depend on God's grace to stand the tests of life, grace will help you to heal. You must be a participant with grace; you must be willing to ask for grace. God waits for us to act first, then He intercedes.

God puts pressure on us to make us perform. God has to test you before you can have a testimony. God will break, mold, and make you over.

Remember that God is in control. The devil cannot do anything in your life without God's permission. God will sometimes allow the devil to bring you hard times, storms, pain, and sickness. After you have made it through "the storm", such enduring yields another testimony of God. God wants everyone to be at peace and full of praise. Give your praise to the Lord because God's grace, love, and mercy are everlasting.

KEY POINT: God's grace is abundant.

QUESTIONS TO ASK YOURSELF:

1. How has God's grace shined on you?

2. Have there been times when you felt God's grace passed you by? If so, how did you deal with this? If not, explain.

_____
_____
_____

3. Do you praise God through all of your circumstances? If yes, explain. If not, what stops you from giving Him praise?

_____
_____
_____

ADDITIONAL SELF-REFLECTION:
What's on Your Mind?

_____
_____
_____
_____
_____

About My Father's Business

IT'S TIME FOR A CHANGE

"East of the Jordan in the territory of Moab, Moses began to expound this law, saying: The Lord our God said to us at Horeb, "You have stayed long enough at this mountain. Break camp and advance into the hill country of the Amorites; go to all the neighboring peoples in the Arabah, in the mountains, in the western foothills, in the Negev and along the coast, to the land of the Canaanites and to Lebanon, as far as the great river, the Euphrates. See, I have given you this land, Go in and take possession of the land that the Lord swore he would give to your fathers - to Abraham, Isaac and Jacob - and to their descendents after them.""

Deuteronomy 1:5-8

Moses told the Israelites that it was time to move from the mountain they had become accustomed to living in, and move to the land the Lord had promised their ancestors. But the people wanted to stay.

Change is an unavoidable part of life. If nothing changed, we would be super bored. Change brings about intrusions into your comfort zones. Everyone and everything, like society, is in motion, all the time. Change is not a choice. How you choose to handle the change is the choice. Change is all around you.

Israel was refusing to change. God had done miracles at the mountain of Sinai but the Israelites kept talking about what God had done in the past, forgetting the current miracles and His ongoing provision for them. God is the same, but mortals are not. The enemy is subtle, slick, and will stage complacency. While mortals wait around for God to do something else, God is waiting for you to do something about what He has already done or what He has already given.

Satan will take the good and the godly and lift it to a place where it will compete with God and try to out do God. God's plan was not for the people to stay at Sinai but to do something and move on from Sinai. Don't lose your focus on why God does things. Don't get caught up in what God "has done". Think about what He wants you to do now. It's not enough to read God's word, pray, or hear God. Ask yourself, what is He doing right now? What have you done since? Where there is divine revelation, there is divine expectation.

Now that you have seen, heard, and studied God's word, it's time for a change. God has got things for you to do but you won't receive these things unless you change. You kill your blessings when you stay complacent in your routines and accept what you think should be normal. Basically, you are just going through the motions.

Some people wonder, where is the Holy Ghost, the power, and the relevance? God's people are supposed to grow. If something does not grow, it will not change. If it does not change, it will not live. If it does not live, then it will not last. If it does not last, it was not God.

About My Father's Business

There are three enemies against change:

1. <u>Rote</u> – The repetition without relevance. Doing something over and over again without thought.

2. <u>Rut</u> – Bondage to the rote. That is, the rote becomes lord. When you want to open yourself to God, and something pulls you back to what you have been doing over and over again, you are in a rut. The danger is when you don't recognize the rut. Jesus sent the Holy Ghost to keep us out of our ruts. It's time for a change.

3. <u>Rot</u> – The inability to accept change. People can dry rot if their leaders are in a rut. You need the word of God in your life. You need His change.

Jesus died, rose up and took all power in His hands. We need His power not to go back into the rut. We need power to keep going, walking in the Holy Ghost. The Holy Ghost shall make us witnesses in overcoming the rut. How do you escape the three enemies against change? You turn, take, and go.

1. <u>Turn</u> – You will be surprised what the Holy Ghost will do if you turn (i.e., change). After you turn, take.

2. <u>Take</u> – God has a purpose for you turning. He wants you to take what He has for you. Then, go.

3. <u>Go</u> – You might have to cut loose some folks who won't turn. But don't worry; your blessing is in front of you. Go, move, and run to your blessing!

The word of God shall be passed on through the generations. When you go, don't be afraid. Don't think small, and don't fall under the rule of routine. Think of your biggest dream and believe that God has planned one even bigger than you could ever imagine. Be fierce and determined in your pursuit. Trust in the Lord that He will carry you through to victory. Allow yourself to express the creativity that God has placed in you. Believe that you are able to achieve all things because God promised that He would deliver you.

> **KEY POINT:** Learn to manage change.

QUESTIONS TO ASK YOURSELF:

1. How well have you managed change when it occurred? What spiritual enhancements can you make to handle change better in the future?

_____
_____
_____

2. What causes you to live in the past? What motivates you to live in the present?

_____
_____
_____

3. What is your greatest dream? What do you think God wants you to do with your life in pursuit of that dream?

_____
_____
_____

About My Father's Business

A BETTER DAY

"He went to Nazareth, where he had been brought up, and on the Sabbath day he went into the synagogue, as was his custom. And he stood up to read. The scroll of the prophet Isaiah was handed to him. Unrolling it, he found the place where it is written: "The Spirit of the Lord is on me, because he has anointed me to preach good news to the poor. He has sent me to proclaim freedom for the prisoners and recovery of sight for the blind, to release the oppressed, to proclaim the year of the Lord's favor." Then he rolled up the scroll, gave it back to the attendant and sat down. The eyes of everyone in the synagogue were fastened on him, and he began by saying to them, "Today this scripture is fulfilled in your hearing."
Luke 4:16-21

Janice N. Adams

At the beginning of His ministry, Jesus entered a synagogue in Nazareth (his hometown), read from the scroll of the prophet Isaiah, and informed all that attended that the scripture had been fulfilled. That is, He claimed that He was anointed to heal broken hearts, to preach the good news to the poor, and to free the imprisoned (be it of the mind, body, or soul), to restore sight to the blind, literally and physically, and to release the oppressed and proclaim the year of God's favor. The people in the synagogue became angry with Jesus because He professed these things but would not do miracles in His hometown like He did elsewhere in the region.

The year of Jubilee is here. Jubilee is a celebration, a rejoicing, and a genuine celebration of liberty. Jesus taught the acceptable year must be pleasing to God. This year should be a year of jubilee, a year of doing not just talking.

Grace and truth came by Jesus. Christ is greater than the angels for the gospels proclaim that even the angels bow down to Him. He was the ultimate sacrifice from God for us. Jesus died at Calvary for our sins. Today, Christ wants to supply your every need. It's time to have a better day. Give your life to Jesus Christ. God has declared that all power of heaven and earth are in His hands. You can't really rejoice until you have given yourself to Christ.

KEY POINT: Rejoice in the Lord.

QUESTIONS TO ASK YOURSELF:

1. How have you celebrated all that Christ has done for you?

About My Father's Business

_____
_____
_____

2. What will you do this year that is pleasing to God?

_____
_____
_____

3. What are you looking forward to in your year of Jubilee?

_____
_____
_____

YOUR EMOTIONS:
*How do you feel right now?
Why do you feel this way?*

_____
_____
_____

Janice N. Adams

SO GREAT SALVATION

"We must pay more careful attention, therefore, to what we have heard, so that we do not drift away. For if the message spoken by angels was binding, and every violation and disobedience received its just punishment, how shall we escape if we ignore such a great salvation? This salvation, which was first announced by the Lord, was confirmed to us by those who heard him. God also testified to it by signs, wonders and various miracles, and gifts of the Holy Spirit distributed according to his will."
Hebrews 2:1-4

The book of Hebrews is saying that we ought to pay attention to what God tells us. We were warned about God's judgment against sinners and His salvation by the angels and prophets like Jeremiah and Isaiah, but people ignored them. So, God sent His message by Jesus Christ (the Gospel). Jesus is far superior to everything and everyone that we know. He is greater than the angels and the old priesthood (i.e., the Old Testament). He became the sacrifice for mankind, once and for all. The old covenants were written on stone, but the new covenants are written in our hearts. If we neglect the salvation that Jesus brought us, then our journey in life will be spent down many twisted roads.

Jesus is the imprint of God's perfect image. Moses brought the laws, but grace (God's free gift of favor and truth) came through Jesus. Through God, Jesus humbled Himself and took on flesh and became man, but a perfect man, to secure our salvation.

Three reasons for Christ's death:

1. <u>Identify with humanity</u>. Since people were made of flesh and blood, Jesus shared in their humanity.

2. <u>Destroy the power of death</u>. Jesus destroyed the devil's hold over people who feared death.

3. <u>Intercessory power of priests</u>. Jesus became a merciful and faithful high priest in service to God after He made atonement for the sins of the people.

Don't neglect what Jesus has done for you. Keep your spirit and body clear so that Jesus will have a clean place to enter. Don't take salvation lightly. He suffered for us greatly. When we fail to remember and honor Jesus, we make His death in vain. Jesus is coming back not as a baby or one who walks among us, but as a ruler, king of kings and Lord of Lords. He will continue to rule. Those who praise Him will be among the saints with Him and will have everlasting life. All the power of heaven and earth is in Jesus' hands. Christ is the perfect model for you to imitate.

> **KEY POINT:** Jesus secured Christian salvation.

QUESTIONS TO ASK YOURSELF:

1. How have you paid homage to Jesus Christ for sacrificing his life so that you and others may have salvation?
   _____
   _____
   _____

2. How often do you think about the sacrifice of Jesus? How does His suffering make you feel?
   _____
   _____
   _____

3. Have you given your life to Christ? Why or why not?
   _____
   _____
   _____

About My Father's Business

SEIZE YOUR MOMENT

"On the day the Lord gave the Amorites over to Israel, Joshua said to the Lord in the presence of Israel: "O sun, stand still over Gibeon, O moon, over the Valley of Aijalon." So the sun stood still, and the moon stopped till the nation avenged itself on its enemies, as it is written in the Book of Jashar. The sun stopped in the middle of the sky and delayed going down about a full day. There has never been a day like it before or since, a day when the Lord listened to a man. Surely the Lord was fighting for Israel! Then Joshua returned with all Israel to the camp at Gilgal."

Joshua 10:12-15

To grab is to take advantage of what is presented to you. Time is of the essence. It only takes a minute to change your life. What you do with your minutes will determine what happens with your life. Use your time wisely. Time and minutes are equal for everyone. The difference is what you do with your time. The "magnificent minute" is the moment that will change your life forever. A minute is the starting point of building your life. Cherish your minutes and use them wisely. How tiny a minute is but eternity dwells within each of those sixty seconds. For example, by praying to God during battle, Joshua was able to stop time and then proceeded to win the battle against five kings whose armies out numbered him.

God is able to do everything without fail. Continue to praise Him. Seize the moment, your moment, and trust God.

KEY POINT: Time is precious; use it wisely.

QUESTIONS TO ASK YOURSELF:

1. How will you react when faced with your magnificent minute?

2. How much do you trust God to bring about the necessary changes in your life so you can seize your special moment?

3. What situations have you taken advantage of that benefited you?

_____
_____
_____

ADDITIONAL SELF-REFLECTION:
What's on Your Mind?

_____
_____
_____
_____
_____

Janice N. Adams

GO DEEP

"Not that I have already obtained all this, or have already been made perfect, but I press on to take hold of that for which Christ Jesus took hold of me. Brothers, I do not consider myself yet to have taken hold of it. But one thing I do: Forgetting what is behind and straining toward what is ahead, I press on toward the goal to win the prize for which God has called me heavenward in Christ Jesus."
Philippians 3:12-14

"Then you will call, and the Lord will answer; you will cry for help, and he will say: Here am I. "If you do away with the yoke of oppression, with the pointing of the finger and malicious talk, and if you spend yourselves in behalf of the hungry and satisfy the needs of the oppressed, then your light will rise in the darkness, and your night will become like the noonday."
Isaiah 58:9-10

About My Father's Business

Study the word of God and press on. Take hold of Jesus Christ. Forget the past and press on to what's ahead of you. Eagerly pursue Jesus Christ, because He has all power and controls all things. Seek Him and He will transform you into a better person. Praise and worship God. Do so through prayer and fasting. Prayer and fasting come easier when you praise and worship God.

How should you pray? Be specific with your prayers. Be truthful, because God already knows your heart and thoughts. He's waiting for you to acknowledge that which you request or confess (For assistance with structuring your prayers, refer to Appendix 2, Prayer Tables on pages 83-84). Prayer is your communication with God. It should be as natural as speaking to your best friend. Prayer should be a daily commitment and practice.

Why fast? You should fast to obtain a state of physiological rest. Fasting brings you closer to God because you are denying your flesh during your fasting period. Fasting is also a way of examination. By cleansing yourself of unnecessary thoughts, you become more focused and are better able to receive messages from the Lord. In the book of Isaiah, chapter fifty-eight explains the promises of God that you will receive when you fast.

> **KEY POINT:** Prayer and fasting cleanses the mind and body.

QUESTIONS TO ASK YOURSELF:

1. *How often do you fast and pray? For what reasons do you fast and pray?*

2. What changes, if any, have you noticed when you fast? How did the experience enlighten you?

3. If you do not practice fasting, what method do you use to reach a deep, spiritual connection with God?

YOUR EMOTIONS:
How do you feel right now?
Why do you feel this way?

About My Father's Business

A SHEPHERD ON A MISSION

"The Lord is my shepherd, I shall not be in want. He makes me lie down in green pastures, he leads me beside quiet waters, he restores my soul. He guides me in paths of righteousness for his name's sake. Even though I walk through the valley of the shadow of death, I will fear no evil, for you are with me; your rod and your staff they comfort me. You prepare a table before me in the presence of my enemies. You anoint my head with oil; my cup overflows. Surely goodness and love will follow me all the days of my life, and I will dwell in the house of the Lord forever."
Psalm 23:1-6

Janice N. Adams

Psalm 23 is not about dying but about how best to live your life while you are in the land of the living. The Psalm promises that you will not lack food, a guide, or protection because the Shepherd provides them.

Jesus leads the way. It is our job to follow. You have to be willing to be guided. Understand that with blessings, come greater responsibility. There is a price to pay for what you are given. The Shepherd has a purpose for each blessing that you're given and the burdens that may come with them. The Shepherd will not give you a vision and not give you the provisions to make it happen. If you stay on the path of righteousness, it might be difficult at times but it will always be right.

The Shepherd takes His sheep through a process but always leads them to a place of peace. Once you accept God's peace, restoration will follow. Ask for His peace because it surpasses all understanding. Trial and tribulations test us, and prepare us to walk in the path of righteousness in His namesake. Lean on Jesus everywhere you go. Don't fear because the Shepherd feeds, guides, and shields. Say aloud, "I am confident and will not fear because I am a child of God." God is always with you and gives you strength to move forward.

God allows an enemy to come next to you to refine you for your next step. Don't allow the enemy to keep you from what you are supposed to do. Be willing to do what God wants you to do. Once you know you are with the Shepherd, His mercy, goodness, love, and kindness will follow you all the days of your life.

The Shepherd is on a mission for you. The question is, are you on a mission for Him? If you step out on your own, without His guidance, circumstances (i.e., the devil) may get the best of you. Therefore, stay in the presence of God, not in the proximity of God. There is only one way to get to God and that is through His son, Jesus Christ.

About My Father's Business

God already knows your destination, and allows situations to occur that you may not understand; but He knows what lies ahead. For example, if you lose your job, God already knows it was being reorganized. He is giving you an opportunity to see and do something else. Pay attention to the Shepherd and He will direct your path. A way will be made clear for you that will bring you into great favor. Follow the Shepherd because He is on a mission for you.

> **KEY POINT:** Have confidence in the Lord.

QUESTIONS TO ASK YOURSELF:

1. What signs do you notice when God is leading you?

2. How righteous is your path? How difficult has venturing down this path been for you?

3. When have you stepped out on faith and let God lead you? What fears did you put aside in order to move forward to the destination God has for you?

Janice N. Adams

RESOLVING FAMILY CONFLICT

"They have moved on from here," the man answered. "I heard them say, 'Let's go to Dothan.'" So Joseph went after his brothers and found them near Dothan. But they saw him in the distance and before he reached them, they plotted to kill him. "Here comes that dreamer!" they said to each other. "Come now, let's kill him and throw him into one of these cisterns and say that a ferocious animal devoured him. Then we'll see what comes of his dreams." When Reuben heard this, he tried to rescue him from their hands. "Let's not take his life," he said. "Don't shed any blood. Throw him into this cistern here in the desert, but don't lay a hand on him." Reuben said this to rescue him from them and take him back to his father."

Genesis 37:17-22

"Do not fret because of evil men or be envious of those who do wrong; for like the grass they will soon wither, like green plants they will soon die away. Trust in the Lord and do good; dwell in the land and enjoy safe pasture. Delight yourself in the Lord and he will give you the desires of your heart."

Psalms 37:1-4

About My Father's Business

Conflict will always exist because we are human. We each have wants, needs, and goals. When these differ or clash with the goals of people around us, conflict may occur. Conflict may also occur independent of others. For example, people sometimes get frustrated with themselves because they don't have the things that they want. In some cases, we don't have what we want because we don't ask God. But understand that it not the lacking that causes the conflict, it is our reaction to these things that drive conflict. Every conflict is an opportunity to control your reactions. Here are five common ways to deal with conflict:

1. Withdraw physically or psychologically.
2. Take a leadership position to resolve conflict.
3. Choose to yield; give in to get along.
4. Compromise; give a little to get a little.
5. Have open and direct communication.

Look at the story of Joseph in Genesis. Jacob loved Joseph because he was the first son of the woman Jacob really loved, Rachel. Therefore, Joseph was his father's favorite child. Jacob made Joseph a special coat of many colors, and used him as a messenger to report on his other siblings. Joseph did not have to work like the other brothers, and he dreamed that his siblings would some day bow down to him. Many of Joseph's brothers were jealous and wanted to kill him. But one brother, Reuben, did not; instead, Reuben reasoned with his brothers that it was not right to kill Joseph, and suggested a compromise that they put him into a pit. The brothers agreed, and Reuben withdrew from the group as they forced Joseph into the pit.

An Ishmaelite caravan came along and Joseph's brother Judah, who wanted to win at any cost, decided to give Joseph to the Ishmaelite. He sold Joseph for 20 pieces of silver ($2,500). In turn, the Ishmaelite sold Joseph into Egypt, and he eventually became Pharaoh's assistant. This made Joseph second in command over all Egypt. When the brothers later met him in Egypt, they feared him because of his power. But Joseph forgave his brothers and declared that what they did to harm him had actually served a greater purpose and was a blessing. Joseph believed that God used his brothers to lead him into his God given purpose.

We have a choice in how we deal with conflict; the word of God shows us the best way.

David dealt with conflict too. God blessed David and made him a commander under King Saul. But Saul soon became jealous, and tried to kill David when the people paid more attention to David and applauded his victories more than Saul's.

In Psalm 37, we see God's approach to conflict. David tells us not to fret of evil men or be envious of those who do wrong because they will be struck down. Instead, trust in the Lord and He will give you the desires of your heart. Rest in the Lord. Don't fret or get angry because it causes you bodily harm.

As a blessing, pray for your family. Encourage one another when you are besieged, and God will strengthen your heart. Love one another and be kind to all persons. When others hurt you, don't pass judgment on them, whether it is your boss, a friend, and/or a family member. If you do, then you are out of alignment with God and this will lead to trouble because God will judge you as you judged others. Remove judgment, send out love, forgive those that hurt you, and stay focused on God's will.

KEY POINT: Control reactions during conflicts.

QUESTIONS TO ASK YOURSELF:

1. What reactions do you display when you are in the midst

About My Father's Business

of conflict with family, friends, or others?

_____
_____
_____

2. What emotion do you feel the most when faced with conflict? When you express this emotion how does it make you feel?

_____
_____
_____

3. Are you willing to try God's solution to conflict, even if it is a difficult change for you? Why or why not?

_____
_____
_____

ADDITIONAL SELF-REFLECTION:
What's on Your Mind?

_____
_____
_____

Janice N. Adams

IT'S TIME TO EAT

"Another of his disciples, Andrew, Simon Peter's brother, spoke up, "Here is a boy with five small barley loaves and two small fish, but how far will they go among so many?" Jesus said, "Have the people sit down." There was plenty of grass in that place, and the men sat down, about five thousand of them. Jesus then took the loaves, gave thanks, and distributed to those who were seated as much as they wanted. He did the same with the fish. When they had all had enough to eat, he said to his disciples, "Gather the pieces that are left over. Let nothing be wasted." So they gathered them and filled twelve baskets with the pieces of the five barely loaves left over by those who had eaten."

John 6:8-13

About My Father's Business

Jesus fed the masses with two fish and five loaves of bread. Bread was given to them to sustain their bodies, but He offered Himself (the body of Christ) as the spiritual bread of life to believers. He freed people from their physical needs first, and then addressed their spiritual needs. God fulfills your natural need first so you will trust Him and follow Him in the supernatural. When God puts His hands on something, it's glorious and marvelous. The old adage is true; you are what you eat, so feast on God and you will have everything you need to survive.

If you eat negative thoughts, complaints and bitterness, you will become all those things. If you feed on God, you will be filled positive thoughts and good deeds. When you feast on Jesus and He resides in you, you will be set apart from the world. To walk with someone means there is an agreement between you and the other person. Ask yourself, are you walking with brothers and sisters in Christ? What are you chewing on other than Christ? Check yourself to be sure you are feeding on Christ and make sure God is your center.

Get back on track by recognizing that God is your answer. Taste and see that the Lord is good. Allow Jesus to abide on the inside of you. Drink and eat of Him, His truth, His faith, and His mercy. Nobody is stopping you from getting your feast. The table is always set and always ready for you to eat with Jesus. It's time to feast on the Holy of Holies.

KEY POINT: Positive thoughts result in positive actions.

QUESTIONS TO ASK YOURSELF:

1. Are your thoughts positive and productive, or negative and

destructive? What impact are your thoughts having on your life?

_____
_____
_____

2. What type of people do you surround yourself with (e.g., positive, optimistic, sarcastic, pessimistic, etc.)? Why do you choose these types of people?

_____
_____
_____

3. What is at the center of your thoughts (e.g., love, trust, goodness, regret, guilt, anger, hurt, etc.)? Why is this the center of your thoughts?

_____
_____
_____

YOUR EMOTIONS:
How do you feel right now?
Why do you feel this way?

_____
_____

About My Father's Business

HARD BUT NOT IMPOSSIBLE

"The disciples were amazed at his words. But Jesus said again, "Children, how hard it is to enter the kingdom of God! It is easier for a camel to go through the eye of a needle than for a rich man to enter the kingdom of God." The disciples were even more amazed, and said to each other, "Who then can be saved?" Jesus looked a them and said, "With man this is impossible, but not with God; all things are possible with God.""
Mark 10:24 – 27

The difficult tasks we often do immediately. The impossible tasks often take a little longer. Just because things are hard doesn't mean they are impossible. If you have a hard thing in your life, turn it over to God. He will make it a possibility. Life can be difficult when you are separated from God. Once you admit this, you've already overcome the difficulty.

Personal growth is arduous; it's a life long task of becoming who God wants you to become. Being lazy makes your growth even more difficult. Too many times we make a promise or New Year's resolution that we seldom keep because we lack a spiritual reformation and renewal. Talk to God about those things you can't tolerate anymore. Stop trying to do things by yourself, and work with God.

Remember, God can judge you even if you haven't done anything bad; He may judge you because you haven't done anything good either. Submit to a spiritual transformation and let the Lord handle one thing you can't handle in life. Breaking bad habits is hard, but not impossible. First identify the one thing in need of change then get some support. The only right support is Jesus. He will be by your side through thick and thin and guide you to the resources you need. Here are a few of God's past successes and references:

- <u>Moses</u> – Pharaoh's army was behind God's chosen people, the Red Sea was in front of them, and Mountains were to the side of them. They had no place to go except forward. God opened the sea so they could pass and wiped out Pharaoh's army who pursued them.

- <u>Joshua</u> –The people of Jericho built a high wall to protect their city, but the Lord was with Joshua. Joshua and his army marched around Jericho six times and on the seventh shout, the walls came tumbling down, leading Joshua and his army to victory.

- <u>Man by the pool</u> – God performed a miracle. He gave sight to a blind man.

If you have a will, God has a way. God can do anything, and His grace will take you through anything. God is your personal trainer. We must be like God and see the end from the beginning. See yourself at the end of what you need and with God's help you shall receive it. The Lord shall make you free, no longer shall chains hold you. If you want to be free, go to Jesus. Don't be in the same place you are today in the coming year.

KEY POINT: The impossible is possible.

QUESTIONS TO ASK YOURSELF:

1. *How have you stayed connected with God so that impossible tasks are possible to overcome?*
___
___
___

2. *What is in your life right now that seems impossible to handle? When will you turned it over to God?*
___
___
___

3. *What spiritual transformation has occurred in your life?*
___
___
___

Janice N. Adams

THE RESURRECTION OF CHRIST

"For what I received I passed on to you as of first importance: that Christ died for our sins according to the Scriptures, that he was buried, that he was raised on the third day according to the Scriptures, and that he appeared to Peter, and then to the Twelve. After that he appeared to more than five hundred of the brothers at the same time, most of whom are still living, though some have fallen asleep. Then he appeared to James, then to all the apostles, and last of all he appeared to me also, as to one abnormally born."
1 Corinthians 15:3-8

First Corinthians covers the facts about the resurrection of Christ as written by the Apostle Paul. He addresses the resurrection from two points of view, one negative and the other positive. Paul explains what life would be like if Christ had not risen from the cross, as well as how life is because He has risen.

About My Father's Business

<u>Negative Points</u> – (Life Without the Resurrected Christ)

- Christ would still be in the grave.
- Christ would be a liar.
- There would be no hope for us to sit on the right and left hand of God.
- The Apostles' preaching would be in vain.
- Our faith would be in vain.
- We would be found false witnesses of Christ. Belief in life after death would be worthless.
- The Christian experience would be imagination.
- We would still be trapped in our sins.
- Preachers would be pitied.
- We would perish like animals.
- Christians would be the most miserable.

Paul then shares what life is like for believers as a result of Christ's resurrection.

<u>Positive Points</u> – (Life With the Resurrected Christ)

- Christ is the first fruit of those who know for certain that all is well. He died for our sins. He was the one perfect lamb sacrificed. He is the first of all believers to testify to the Father, the Son, and the Holy Spirit. He is God's only begotten son. Through Him, others may come to know and believe in the Trinity of the Father, Son, and Holy Ghost.
- Christ appeared to dozens of people after His resurrection. He proved that He had conquered death and showed all of us that He was who He said that He was (the Son of God), and that He holds all power in His hands.
- He brought joy, and made it possible for us to receive the Holy Ghost.

The Resurrection is the key to our faith. It is the foundation and corner stone of our Christian belief, based on the word of God. Do you recognize Jesus and the resurrection of Christ in your life?

Recognize the power of the Resurrection at work when Christ heals your body, when He provides, and when He touches your soul so you can have a relationship with God. Believe that Jesus conquered death and is alive, that He lives forever more. Therefore, you ought to have joy in your heart and no fear of death. If Christ had not died for us on Calvary, you would have no hope for eternal life. But because He did, you have a relationship with God as a gift. All you have to do is believe in the Lord Jesus and you shall have eternal life.

When you have burdens and hardships, talk to the Lord and let the Lord speak to you. Pray for God to grant you the wisdom and understanding that you need. He will enlighten you. We know Christ lives because He lives in our hearts. Has Christ appeared unto you? Does He live in your heart?

If you don't think He has appeared in your life yet, continue to seek Him. Jesus wants to spend time with you personally. Will you seek Him? He is not dead. He lives and lives forever more. Both the historical evidence and countless changed lives prove to us that Christ is alive today.

KEY POINT: Eternal life is offered through Jesus Christ.

QUESTIONS TO ASK YOURSELF:

1. Do you believe that Jesus is alive with all power in His hands? Why or why not?

___

___

About My Father's Business

2. When will you open your heart and mind to receive God's perfect gift, Jesus Christ?

_____
_____

3. What burdens and hardships would you talk about to the Lord today to receive His help?

_____
_____
_____

ADDITIONAL SELF-REFLECTION:
What's on Your Mind?

_____
_____
_____
_____
_____

I WOKE UP THIS MORNING

"After his suffering, he showed himself to these men and gave many convincing proofs that he was alive. He appeared to them over a period of forty days and spoke about the kingdom of God."
Acts 1:3

Being alive in the world but asleep in your spirit is not good. Forty is the number of revival. Jesus appeared to the Apostles for forty days after His resurrection and spoke to them about the kingdom of God. Revival is reawakening to divine possibility. God gave the apostles forty days of revival. God showed them that just because Jesus had been crucified, the matter was not over. God continued to show His love for mankind by giving them the Holy Spirit.

Love is the power to reunite that, which is broken. A revival suggests trial. You can't have a revival without going through something challenging. Revival gives you the power to walk through the challenge. Ask for the strength to hold on, hang in there, and let the Lord use you. Challenges teach you how to pray and strengthen you. You ought to write the enemy a thank you letter because the situation that you were dealing with taught you how to pray.

Greater is He that is in you than he that is in the world. There is a will in the heart of man. There should be a fire in your bones. If you wake up feeling down, know there should be joy in your soul because Jesus is alive and has already suffered for you. God will pick you up and turn you around because God is able. Your praise is your joy. Give God praise if you believe He is able and good. Take ten seconds and give God praise. Every morning you should be thankful and express your gratitude.

KEY POINT: Perseverance strengthens.

QUESTIONS TO ASK YOURSELF:

1. From what source do you get your strength, when challenges arise?

_____
_____

2. What situation(s) did you overcome that has made you internally stronger?

_____
_____

3. What advice would you give others to persevere over their circumstances? How is your advice aligned with God's will?

_____
_____
_____

YOUR EMOTIONS:
*How do you feel right now?
Why do you feel this way?*

_____
_____
_____

MARCHING FEET IN THE TREETOPS

"Once more the Philistines came up and spread out in the Valley of Rephaim; so David inquired of the Lord, and he answered. "Do not go straight up, but circle around behind them and attack them in front of the balsam trees. As soon as you hear the sound of marching in the tops of the balsam trees, move quickly, because that will mean the Lord has gone out in front of you to strike the Philistine army." So David did as the Lord commanded him, and he struck down the Philistines all the way from Gibeon to Gezer."
II Samuel 5:22-25

David was made king over the chosen nation of Israel. When the Lord raises you to a new field of labor, it won't take Satan long to come along and try to sabotage you, just as the Philistines tried to capture David. That's why it's important to stay with God. When the enemy shows you their armor and threatens you, pray to God; He can defeat every snare of the enemy for you, if you follow His plan. You will be victorious every time.

You pick your place to fight your battle. David attacked the Philistines from the rear and not head on because God told him what to do once David prayed. Request of God how you should attack the enemy so that He will lead you into victory. Like David, when you hear God sending marching feet in the treetops, know that God has gone out in front of you. Attack like God tells you. Something moves you on the inside when you're stepping with God. The Lord still has an army in the treetops. You will hear the voice of God telling you to fight on and He'll give you the strength. God is in the front of your battle. He will make sure victory is gained. When you hear God in His glory and fullness, you can say, "Up above my head I hear music in the air. There's a God somewhere." We need to get in step with the feet in the treetops. That is to say, we need to get in step with God's orders and let Him guide us.

KEY POINT: Let God guide you through your battles.

QUESTIONS TO ASK YOURSELF:

1. What are the results of your battles in life when you fight them by yourself without God's guidance?

2. How willing are you to be patient and allow God to intercede?

About My Father's Business

_____
_____
_____

3. How will you face your battles in the future? What is different about this approach than before?

_____
_____
_____

ADDITIONAL SELF-REFLECTION:
What's on Your Mind?

_____
_____
_____
_____
_____

Janice N. Adams

ANTIDOTE FOR ANXIETY

"Do not be anxious about anything, but in everything, by prayer and petition with thanksgiving, present your requests to God. And the peace of God, which transcends all understanding will guard your hearts and your minds in Christ Jesus."
Philippians 4:6-9

"Do you not know? The Lord is the everlasting God, the Creator of the ends of the earth. He will not grow tired or weary, and his understanding no one can fathom. He gives strength to the weary and increases the power of the weak. Even youths grow tired and weary, and young men stumble and fall; but those who hope in the Lord will renew their strength."
Isaiah 40:28-31

About My Father's Business

"Do not conform any longer to the pattern of this world, but be transformed by the renewing of your mind. Then you will be able to test and approve what God's will is - his good, pleasing and perfect will."
Romans 12:2

God knows what we need, and has already provided us an antidote for anxiety; it is our memory. We should be remembering things related to God.
When you receive bad news or have challenges, turn it over to God. When you worry, focus on God and His peace to relax your mind and soul. Let your mind be transformed. Remember, God has the answer. Renewing the mind allows your thoughts to be transitioned into a better way of thinking. Jesus was in full control because He allowed His thoughts to be fixated on God's will, even though His people were crucifying Him. Jesus was not anxious, neither should you be as a believer.

There are six things about God that you should remember that are an antidote for anxiety.

1. <u>God is Infinite</u>. He is Alpha and Omega. People and circumstances are finite. Why worry when you can put your challenges in the hands of the infinite? Whatever you are going through, God has been there and done that. Knowing this ought to bring your stress down because He will give you what you need to handle your situation if you trust Him.

2. <u>God is Independent</u>. He existed before everything that is. He's God by Himself. People need Him. He's independent in His way, His work, in anything He chooses. He can do whatever He wants because He is Lord. Even the devil has to depend on God (when the devil challenges you). Don't talk to the devil to rebuke him, talk to God. God can and will handle the devil. God saves those who Love Him. He will rescue and

protect those who acknowledge Him. God's grace is abundant.

3. <u>God is Innovative</u>. God created the ends of the earth. He took Adam and made all the nationalities. Man can only create out of pre-existing materials. In Genesis, God thought first and then He created light and separated it from the darkness. When it looks like checkmate, God is so innovative that He makes a way out of no way. Stand still and receive the salvation of God because He is an innovator when He saves people. Remember how he saved Moses and the Israelites crossing the Red Sea when Pharaoh's army was behind them? God will save you too. When you think you're going away from Him, He'll be right where you thought He wouldn't be, like Jonah in the whale. Religion is man's attempt to get closer to God. Remember that God is interested in establishing personal relationships with mankind. God is so innovative that He made Himself to be born to a virgin in order to offer Himself to mankind as their savior.

4. <u>God is Infatiguable</u>. God never gets tired. He never gets tired of forgiving and never walks away from us. He doesn't get tired of fighting for you. If God be for you, who can be against you? He's stronger than any force against you. God will always exceed your needs. He does exceedingly and abundantly more than what you could ask of Him.

5. <u>God is Incomprehensible</u>. Man tries to make sense of God but God doesn't want man's understanding. He wants your faith. He's omni first. He knows everything from beginning to end. God knows all and sees all, even in the dark. God is omnipresent. God is with you always. He has all power in His hands.

6. <u>God is Invigorating</u>. He gives people strength to go on one more time, and He will renew your strength. Walk without

becoming weary. Keep your faith because the best is yet to come, and everything is going to be all right. Jesus died and rose again with all power in His hands. Remember that you are able with the Lord.

The enemy tries to impose onto us all those expressions of lack that create such anxiety in our lives; things such as despair, depression, and stress. To rebuke the devil and his mission to destroy the good things in your life, go to God; go to that spiritual place of power within you and request, in Jesus' name, that He rebuke the devil and spoil his efforts.

Understand that you have authority over your circumstances, for God has given you power and dominion over those earthly circumstances that may cause anxiety. However, you must tap into the strength within you, that special place where God resides. Call on the Lord to help you and use the power He has blessed you with already. Renew your mind, because your thoughts control your emotions and actions. So keep your thoughts focused on God, and He will relieve your anxiety.

KEY POINT: Remember how powerful God is in all things.

QUESTIONS TO ASK YOURSELF:

1. What anxiety do you have in your life today?

_____
_____
_____

2. How well are you managing your anxiety?
_____
_____
_____

3. What part of God's greatness do you need to focus on in order to get better control of any anxiety you may have?
_____
_____
_____

YOUR EMOTIONS:
How do you feel right now?
Why do you feel this way?
_____
_____
_____

About My Father's Business

APPENDIX 1: DISCUSSION QUESTIONS

In addition to using these thought provoking questions for you, share them with your book club, friends, and family.

1. What is your spiritual goal? What action can you take today to move toward your goal?

2. In what way, would you like to be more Christ-like in your life?

3. When do you humble yourself to the Lord?

4. What actions cause you to have a heart of repentance? How are you eliminating such actions from your life?

5. What do you like to do (i.e., your special gift or talent) that you can share with others?

6. How have you used wisdom to help you grow spiritually?
_____
_____
_____

7. When people ask or talk to you about the word of God, what do you say or do?
_____
_____
_____

8. Why do you think mankind is deserving of God's grace?
_____
_____
_____

9. When do you need the Lord's loving discipline and self-control the most in your life?
_____
_____
_____

10. From this moment forward, how will you conduct yourself in a way more pleasing to God?
_____
_____
_____

APPENDIX 2: PRAYER TABLES

To help you enhance your communication with your spiritual guide, use the Prayer Tables to structure your thoughts and prayers. Table 1 is designed for your spiritual requests and confessions. Table 2 is designed so that you can outline and express your appreciation.

TABLE 1 – REQUEST OR CONFESSION

DATE:	SPIRITUAL TOPIC:			
	TO WHOM YOU PRAY			
DEAR:	☐ God/Jehovah ☐ Jesus Christ ☐ Holy Spirit		☐ Allah ☐ Muhammad ☐ Creator	☐ Divine Spirit ☐ Other:
THIS IS A:	☐ Request to		☐ Confession to	
	ABOUT WHAT		**FOR WHOM**	
PLEASE:	☐ Change ☐ Fix ☐ Forgive ☐ Provide	☐ Grant ☐ Heal ☐ Help ☐ Other:	☐ Me ☐ My Enemy ☐ My Family ☐ My Friends ☐ Our Leaders	☐ Sinners ☐ The Pain ☐ The Suffering ☐ The World ☐ Other:
BECAUSE:				
FOR YOUR BLESSING, I WILL:				

TABLE 2 – EXPRESSION OF APPRECIATION

DATE:	SPIRITUAL TOPIC:		
DEAR:	**TO WHOM YOU PRAY**		
	☐ God/Jehovah	☐ Allah	☐ Divine Spirit
	☐ Jesus Christ	☐ Muhammad	☐ Other:
	☐ Holy Spirit	☐ Creator	
THIS IS AN EXPRESSION OF:	**ABOUT WHAT**	**FOR YOUR**	
	☐ Gratitude	☐ Goodness	☐ Love
	☐ Appreciation	☐ Grace	☐ Mercy
	☐ Relief	☐ Guidance	☐ Miracle
	☐ Gladness	☐ Kindness	☐ Wisdom
			☐ Other:
BECAUSE OF YOU:			
I AM NOW:			

APPENDIX 3: INTERCESSORY PRAYER LIST

The Intercessory Prayer List is composed of scripture from the NIV Bible that addresses specific topics people face in everyday life. Incorporate the word of God into your daily routine as you continue your spiritual growth.

Consequence of Forgetting God
Hosea 4:1-11

Illness
James 5:13-15

Waiting for Medical Test Results
Deuteronomy 31:8

Facing a Major Decision
Psalm 32:8

Dealing with a Difficult Future
Isaiah 45:2-3

The Greatest Commandment
Matthew 22:36-40

The Value of the Soul
Mark 8:36-37

Do You Believe That I Am Able
Matthew 9:27-29

It's a Brand New Day
Isaiah 60:1-5

Janice N. Adams

Jesus, a Divine Direction Given
Proverbs 1:20-33

Looking at Failure
Psalm 32:1-6

Confidence That God Hears Prayers
I John 5:14-15

Spiritual Coverage for Children
Isaiah 54:13

Awaiting Results from Job Interviews
Jeremiah 32:17, 26, 27

When in Sorrow
John 14

When Men Fail You
Psalm 27

For Security
Psalm 121:3

Assurance
Mark 8:35

Fighting Temptation
Matthew 4:1-11

When You Grow Bitter and Critical
I Corinthians 13

Apostle Paul's Secret to Happiness
Colossians 3:1-17

APPENDIX 4: SPIRITUAL RESOURCES

Listed below are a few suggested websites to visit if you would like additional spiritual information. These resources contain everything from books and newsletters to pod casts, television, and radio ministry broadcasting.

<u>On-line Bible Resources</u>
>www.biblegateway.com
>www.blueletterbible.org
>www.crosswalk.com

<u>Christian Ministries</u>

>Charles Capps Ministries
>www.charlescappsministries.org

>Creflo Dollar Ministries
>www.creflodollarministries.org

>Jessie Duplantis Ministries
>www.jdm.org

>Kenneth Copeland Ministries
>www.kcm.org

>Rick Warren
>www.purposedrivenlife.com

>Trinity Broadcasting Network
>www.TBN.org

Janice N. Adams

APPENDIX 5: REFERENCES

Mount Olive Baptist Church
8775 Mount Olive Avenue, Glen Allen, VA 23060
Michael V. Kelsey, Sr., Senior Pastor

Mount Calvary Baptist Church
608 N. Horners Lane, Rockville, MD, 20850
Reverend Leon Grant, Pastor

The People's Community Baptist Church
31 Norwood Rd., Silver Spring, MD 20905
Dr. Haywood A. Robinson, III, Pastor

New Samaritan Baptist Church
1100 Florida Avenue, NE, Washington, DC 20002
Michael V. Kelsey, Sr., Senior Pastor

Loudon Avenue Christian Church
730 Loudon Avenue, NW, Roanoke, VA 24016
William L. Lee, Pastor

Central Baptist Church
1502 Staunton Avenue, NW, Roanoke, VA 24017
Reverend Dr. Joseph A. Keaton, Pastor

New Friendship Baptist Church
1515 E. Eager Street, Baltimore, MD 21205
Reverend Michael W. Palmer

About the Author

*J*anice *N. Adams* is a published author who ignites life into literary works. Her storylines take your mind away from the daily hustle bustle as you laugh, cry, and cheer for her characters. In 2008, she completed the fiction novel, *A Heart's Journey* and collaborated with *New York Times* bestselling author, Zane to contribute her novella, *A Twisted State of Mind* to Zane's anthology, *Another Time, Another Place*. In 2009, Janice completed two non-fiction books of inspiration, *About My Father's Business* and *About My Father's Footsteps*. She is currently preparing her next installment, *Deep Waters: A Heart's Journey Part Two*. She is the founder and owner of JAVISTA BOOKS, a publishing company she created to develop original stories for print and digital works that uplift the human spirit while entertaining readers with vibrant stories. She earned a Bachelor of Science degree in Sociology from Virginia Polytechnic Institute & State University and has worked over twenty-five years in corporate and government entities in the areas of Information Technology, Human Resources and Program Management. She resides in Maryland and is the proud mother of two sons.

Visit www.janicenadams.com for more information
Follow her on Facebook

www.ingramcontent.com/pod-product-compliance
Lightning Source LLC
Chambersburg PA
CBHW071721040426
42446CB00011B/2156